the *perfectly* dressed salad

the *perfectly dressed* salad

More than 50 recipes to make your salads sing,
from quick-fix vinaigrettes to creamy classics

Louise Pickford

photography by Ian Wallace

RYLAND PETERS & SMALL
LONDON • NEW YORK

I'd like to thank my husband for his never wavering patience at tasting new recipes and his diplomacy when they don't go to plan. I'd like to dedicate this book to my Dad, no longer with us, but never far from our thoughts.

Senior Designer Sonya Nathoo
Commissioning Editor Nathan Joyce
Senior Editor Miriam Catley
Production Meskerem Berhane
Art Director Leslie Harrington
Editorial Director Julia Charles

Food and prop stylist Louise Pickford
Indexer Hilary Bird

First published in 2014 by
Ryland Peters & Small
20–21 Jockey's Fields
London WC1R 4BW
and
519 Broadway, 5th Floor
New York, NY 10012

www.rylandpeters.com

10 9 8 7 6 5 4 3 2 1

Text © Louise Pickford 2014
Design and photographs © Ryland Peters & Small 2014

Printed in China

ISBN: 978-1-84975-498-9

A CIP record for this book is available from the British Library.
US Library of Congress CIP data has been applied for.

Notes
• All spoon measurements are level unless otherwise specified.
• All vegetables are medium-sized unless otherwise specified.
• All eggs are medium (UK) or large (US), unless specified. Uncooked or partially cooked eggs should not be served to the very old, frail, young children, pregnant women or those with compromised immune systems.
• When a recipe calls for the grated zest of citrus fruit, buy unwaxed fruit and wash well before using. If you can only find treated fruit, scrub well in warm soapy water before using.
• Citrus juice should be used freshly squeezed
• If you are making a dressing using nut oils, store the opened oils in the fridge, as they will spoil at room temperature.

contents

introduction

A salad without a dressing would be no salad at all. Of course there are as many dressings as salads so compiling a collection of just 50 was, much like a dressing itself, a balancing act to ensure I managed to cover as many different types of dressings as I could.

Dressings can be divided into two main categories: vinaigrettes – an oil and vinegar dressing lightly whisked together until amalgamated just prior to use – and creamy dressings or emulsions – where oil and vinegar are whisked with another element until thickened permanently. These make up two chapters in this book while a further four chapters, Fruity, Herbed, Warm and Infused Dressings, cover variations of these.

So what is vinaigrette? The word derives from the French 'vinaigre' or 'sour wine'. A vinaigrette generally consists of three parts oil to one part vinegar or citrus (although this will vary according to taste) and can be made using various oils such as olive, walnut, hazelnut, sunflower and grape seed oil. Vinegars, too, vary greatly and include white and red wine vinegar, raspberry and other fruit vinegars, cider vinegar and balsamic vinegar.

Creamy dressings are a mixture of oil and vinegar that require the addition of an emulsifier in order to remain stable. Emulsifying agents include egg and mustard and combine to make such classic dressings as mayonnaise and Caesar salad dressing. Again, creamy dressings are flavoured with various other elements from ketchup and Worcestershire sauce, to herbs and spices as well as finely chopped onions.

In the Fruity Dressings chapter I have included fruit-based vinegars as well as puréed fruits such as mango, a homemade pomegranate syrup and even diced fresh peach dressing. Herbed dressings are flavoured with finely chopped herbs added to a simple oil and vinegar mixture along with cream, mayonnaise or yogurt with additional flavours such as horseradish.

Infused dressings differ slightly as the oil is infused first with herbs, spices or citrus, strained and then blended with vinegar. This gives the oil and subsequently the dressing their underlying flavour and characteristic.

Warm (or cooked) dressings are where the integral ingredients are first heated in a pan to cook them and then vinegar (or citrus juice) and oil are added; the resulting dressing is then poured warm over the salad.

Once made, I feel dressings should be used as soon as they can be – if you do make a vinaigrette ahead of time be sure to blend again just prior to serving. If you are storing any dressings, keep them in a sealed container in the fridge for 2–3 days. Return to room temperature before using and shake well if needed.

The salad suggestions I give in each recipe are guidelines only and you can serve each dressing with any salad you like. As you will discover over the following pages, there is a simply staggering number of wonderful and different dressings, which of course means an equally staggering number of delicious salads.

vinaigrettes

tarragon

When available, use macadamia nut oil in this dressing as it has a mild nutty flavour that really shows off the tarragon to its best. Hazelnut oil is also good and perhaps a more readily available alternative. If you love the flavour of tarragon, use tarragon vinegar.

2 teaspoons white wine vinegar or tarragon vinegar
1 teaspoon Dijon mustard
1/2–1 teaspoon caster/superfine sugar
2 tablespoons chopped fresh tarragon
3 tablespoons macadamia or hazelnut oil
1 tablespoon extra virgin olive oil
salt and pepper

Makes 125 ml/1/2 cup

Place the vinegar, mustard, sugar, tarragon and a little salt and pepper in a blender and blend until combined, then add the oil and blend again until amalgamated. Adjust seasoning to taste and serve.

Serve this dressing over a poached salmon salad.

champagne vinegar

Champagne, like wine, can be used to make vinegar and produces a mild vinegar. It is available from specialist food stores.

2 tablespoons champagne vinegar
6 tablespoons extra virgin olive oil
salt and pepper

Makes 75 ml/1/3 cup

Place the vinegar, oil and some salt and pepper in a screw top jar, seal and shake well until the dressing is amalgamated. Adjust seasoning to taste and serve.

This is delicious served with salad leaves, crumbled goat's cheese and very thinly sliced pears.

Variation: To make your own Champagne vinegar, place 250 ml/1 cup plus 1 tablespoon sparkling white wine in a jar, cover with muslin/cheesecloth and set aside in a cool place for several weeks. Taste from time to time and when the wine has turned to vinegar store in a screw top jar.

sweet chilli

Hot, sweet and sour together is a flavour combination we associate with Asian cuisine and this dressing epitomizes that. Using bird's eye chillies/chiles will result in a fiery dressing so, if you prefer a milder heat, either discard the seeds or use 1 large, mild chilli/chile.

75 ml/¹/₃ cup rice wine vinegar
50 g/¹/₄ cup granulated sugar
2 red bird's eye chillies/chiles, thinly sliced
6 tablespoons peanut oil
juice ¹/₂ lime
2 tablespoons Thai fish sauce
salt

Makes 150 ml/²/₃ cup

Place the vinegar, sugar and 1 tablespoon water in a small saucepan and heat gently to dissolve the sugar, then simmer for 5 minutes until the mixture is syrupy. Stir in the sliced chillies/chiles and allow to cool completely.

Whisk in the remaining ingredients until the dressing is amalgamated and adjust seasoning to taste.

This is wonderful drizzled over a Thai beef salad with tomatoes, cucumber, red onions and fresh herbs.

mild curry

The curry spices are softened with onion, garlic and ginger and then strained so that the resulting oil has a deep curry flavour without the bits. The oil is then whisked with lemon and a little cream, making a wonderfully aromatic dressing.

3 tablespoons sunflower oil
1 small onion, finely chopped
1 garlic clove, crushed
1 teaspoon grated root ginger
1 teaspoon curry powder
2 teaspoons freshly squeezed lemon juice
3 tablespoons extra virgin olive oil
1 tablespoon single/light cream
salt and pepper

Makes 100 ml/¹/₃ cup plus 1 tablespoon

Heat the sunflower oil in a small frying pan/skillet and gently fry the onion, garlic, ginger, curry powder and a little salt and pepper over a low heat for 5 minutes until softened. Strain the mixture through a fine sieve/strainer and set aside to cool.

Stir in the lemon juice and then whisk in the olive oil and cream until smooth and amalgamated. Adjust seasoning to taste and serve.

Serve this with a shredded chicken, celery and walnut salad.

Thai beef salad with
sweet chilli dressing

japanese-style sweet miso and sesame

Miso paste, made from fermented soya beans, is used extensively in Japanese cooking. It is salty, earthy and malty and adds a rich depth of flavour to dishes. Here it is sweetened and combined with sesame oil. You can buy miso paste from Asian stores, health food stores or larger supermarkets – there are several types available but any can be used in this dressing.

2 tablespoons sunflower oil

2 tablespoons rice wine
   vinegar

2 tablespoons miso paste

2 teaspoons caster/superfine
   sugar

2 teaspoon sesame oil

Makes 125 ml/½ cup

Place all the ingredients into a jar and shake well until evenly blended. If the sauce is a little thick, thin slightly by whisking in a teaspoon of water.

   This robust dressing is perfect tossed with cooked noodles, shredded vegetables and topped with toasted sesame seeds.

wasabi, lemon and avocado oil

Wasabi is Japanese horseradish, an integral ingredient in sushi and an accompaniment to sashimi. It adds a wonderful pungency to dishes and is lovely in a salad dressing. Rather than combining it with other traditional Japanese ingredients, here it is whisked with avocado oil and lemon juice for a refreshingly different flavour.

1 teaspoon wasabi paste

**¹/₂ teaspoon caster/superfine
  sugar**

**1 tablespoon lemon or
  lime juice**

3 tablespoons avocado oil

a pinch of salt

Makes 75 ml/⅓ cup

Place the wasabi paste, sugar, lemon or lime juice and the salt in a bowl and, using a small balloon whisk, blend to form a smooth paste. Gradually whisk in the oil until amalgamated and adjust seasoning to taste.

This is delicious drizzled over raw tuna or beef carpaccio or a cooked prawn/shrimp salad.

noodle and tofu salad with
chilli and sesame dressing

chilli and sesame

The base of this dressing is a sweet and savoury syrup made with sugar and rice wine vinegar. The remaining ingredients are then whisked into the cooled syrup. You can use sunflower oil instead of peanut oil if preferred.

2 teaspoons caster/superfine sugar
1 tablespoon rice wine vinegar
1/4 teaspoon salt
1 tablespoon light soy sauce
2–3 tablespoons peanut oil
1–2 teaspoons toasted sesame oil
1 large red chilli/chile, seeded and finely chopped

Makes 150 ml/2/3 cup

Place the sugar, vinegar and salt in a small saucepan with 1 tablespoon of cold water. Heat gently until the sugar dissolves, then increase the heat and simmer for 2 minutes. Remove from the heat, allow to go cold.

Place the cooled mixture in a jar with the remaining ingredients, seal the lid and shake well until evenly blended. Adjust seasoning to taste and serve.

This is fab with a Chinese-style shredded rice noodle, vegetable and tofu salad.

nuoc chum

Nuoc chum is a Vietnamese dipping sauce. It is at once hot, salty, sweet and sour. If you want to increase the fiery nature of the dressing, add the chilli/chile seeds.

1 large red chilli/chile, chopped
1 red bird's eye chilli/chile, seeded and chopped
1 garlic clove, crushed
2 tablespoons grated palm sugar
2 tablespoons Thai fish sauce
grated zest and juice 2 limes
salt and pepper

Makes: 150 ml/2/3 cup

Place the chillies/chiles, garlic and palm sugar in a pestle and mortar (or blender) and pound or blend to form a paste. Transfer to a bowl and whisk in the remaining ingredients.

This is a delicious dressing to toss through a shredded green papaya salad with Vietnamese mint and crushed peanuts.

bloody mary

Using a ripe tomato, rather than tomato juice, in this dressing version of the classic 'day after' pick-me-up adds a refreshing tang to it.

1 ripe tomato, roughly chopped
1 tablespoon vodka
2 teaspoons white wine vinegar
1 teaspoon Worcestershire sauce
a few drops Tabasco
a pinch celery salt
pepper
2 tablespoons extra virgin olive oil
lemon juice, to taste

Makes 125 ml/½ cup

Place the tomato in a blender and add the vodka, vinegar, Worcestershire sauce, Tabasco, celery salt and a little pepper. Blend until smooth, then transfer to a bowl and gradually whisk in the oil until the dressing is emulsified. Add enough lemon juice for your taste and adjust seasoning to taste.

I love to serve this fabulous dressing drizzled over freshly shucked oysters.

smoky barbecue

By char-grilling the chilli/chile, garlic and tomato over a gas flame the smoky flavour permeates the flesh, giving this dressing its distinctive flavour.

1 large red chilli/chile
1 large garlic clove, unpeeled
1 tomato
1 tablespoon red wine vinegar
1 teaspoon Dijon mustard
2 teaspoons Worcestershire sauce
2 teaspoons molasses
½ teaspoon smoked paprika
2 tablespoons extra virgin olive oil
salt and pepper

Makes 200 ml/1 scant cup

Thread the chilli/chile and garlic clove (left unpeeled) onto a metal skewer and char-grill over a gas flame, turning, until evenly charred. Set aside to cool. Using tongs to hold the tomato, char-grill the skin over the flame. Peel the skin from the chilli/chile, garlic and tomato. De-seed the chilli/chile and finely chop the flesh. Crush the garlic clove, de-seed and finely dice the tomato flesh.

Place the tomato, chilli/chile, garlic, vinegar, mustard, Worcestershire sauce, molasses, smoked paprika and a little salt and pepper in a blender and blend until really smooth. Transfer to a bowl and whisk in the oil. Adjust seasoning to taste and serve.

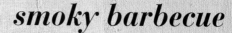

freshly shucked oysters with
bloody mary dressing

walnut and vincotto

Vincotto (cooked wine) is a sweet, dark syrup made from fermented grape must and comes from Apulia in the south of Italy. It is available from Italian delis and specialist food stores.

1 tablespoon vincotto
2 teaspoons red wine vinegar
3 tablespoons walnut oil
1 tablespoon extra virgin olive oil
salt and pepper

Makes 75 ml/⅓ cup

Whisk all the ingredients together, adjust seasoning to taste and serve. Serve drizzled over a tomato and rocket/arugula salad with shavings of aged Parmesan.

hazelnut

A simple vinaigrette that is nonetheless delicious. The raspberry vinegar seems to complement the nut oil beautifully.

2 teaspoons raspberry vinegar
1 teaspoon caster/superfine sugar
4 tablespoons hazelnut oil
salt and pepper

Makes 100 ml/⅓ cup plus 1 tablespoon

Whisk the vinegar, sugar, salt and pepper together and then whisk in the oil until amalgamated. Adjust seasoning to taste. Serve with a green leaf salad.

reduced balsamic

Making your own reduced balsamic vinegar is a great way of transforming an inexpensive vinegar into a fabulous sweet balsamic caramel and, consequently, a delicious vinaigrette. Just be sure to watch the vinegar closely as it reduces as it will easily go too far and become burnt vinegar!

500 ml/17 fl. oz. cheap balsamic vinegar
5 tablespoons extra virgin olive oil
salt and pepper

Makes 100 ml/⅓ cup plus 1 tablespoon

Place the balsamic vinegar in a small pan and simmer over a high heat for about 10 minutes until approximately 150 ml/⅔ cup remains and the vinegar is thick and syrupy. Allow to cool completely.

Combine the oil, cooled reduced balsamic vinegar and salt and pepper together, whisking well, and serve.

This versatile dressing works well on green leaves, any type of tomato salad and is, of course, perfect with a Caprese salad of tomatoes, avocado and mozzarella.

h

The term French dressing is universal but originally it was used to describe a vinaigrette. It is an emulsion of oil and vinegar in varying quantities. Any type of oil can be used, along with an acid of either vinegar or citrus juice. To make a really good French dressing the balance of flavours should be just right – neither too sharp nor too oily. If storing, keep in an airtight container in the fridge for up to 2 days and shake well before using.

**1 tablespoon Chardonnay
white wine vinegar**
1 teaspoon Dijon mustard
a pinch of sugar
**4 tablespoons extra virgin
olive oil**
2 tablespoons sunflower oil
salt and pepper

*Makes 100 ml/⅓ cup plus
1 tablespoon*

In a bowl stir together the vinegar, mustard, sugar, salt and pepper until smooth and then gradually whisk in the oils until amalgamated. Season to taste and serve. Alternatively store in a screw top jar in the fridge for up to 1 week, shaking well before use. Use on any salad of your choice.

mustard

Here Dijon mustard and whole grain mustard are used together to give the dressing both a creamy and a grainy texture, which is perfect on a salad of crisp leaves.

1½ teaspoons Dijon mustard

1½ teaspoons whole grain
   mustard

2 teaspoons red wine vinegar

a pinch of caster/superfine
   sugar

4 tablespoons extra virgin
   olive oil

salt and pepper

*Makes 100 ml/⅓ cup plus
1 tablespoon*

Place the mustards, vinegar, sugar and a little salt and pepper in a bowl and stir well until smooth. Gradually whisk in the oil until the dressing is amalgamated, adjust seasoning to taste and serve.

Variation: For tarragon mustard dressing add 1 tablespoon chopped fresh tarragon to the finished dressing.

creamy dressings

mayonnaise

In order to make mayonnaise you must form a permanent emulsion of two ingredients that ordinarily do not mix together, in this case egg yolks and oil. I like to use half fruity extra virgin olive oil and half pure olive oil to produce a milder flavour.

3 egg yolks
2 teaspoons white wine vinegar or lemon juice
1 teaspoon Dijon mustard
150 ml/²/₃ cup extra virgin olive oil
150 ml/²/₃ cup olive oil
salt and ground white pepper

Makes 300 ml/1¼ cups

Place the egg yolks, vinegar, mustard and a little salt and pepper in a bowl and, using electric beaters, whisk until the mixture is frothy. Then very gradually whisk in the two oils, a little at a time, whisking well after each addition, until the sauce is thickened and glossy and all the oil incorporated. If the mixture is too thick, thin it with a teaspoon or so of boiling water until you reach the required consistency. Adjust seasoning to taste and serve or store.

Variations:
Aïoli – add 2–4 crushed garlic cloves to the mayonnaise and blend until smooth.
Fresh herb – add 1–2 tablespoons roughly chopped herbs to the mayonnaise and blend again briefly until speckled green.

ranch

Named after the dude ranch run by Steve Henson and his wife Gayle in California in the 1950s where they invented a creamy, lightly spiced dressing for the salads they served. It was so popular with guests that they started to make small bottles of it and a ranch spice mix to take away. Its popularity grew to the point that they were soon shipping it all over the States. Today it is the biggest-selling dressing in the US – you will find many different brands available in stores, but, of course, home-made is always the best.

125 ml/¹/₂ cup buttermilk
150 ml/²/₃ cup mayonnaise
1 tablespoon chopped fresh chives
1 tablespoon chopped fresh parsley
1 garlic clove, crushed
1 teaspoon mild American mustard
a few drops of Tabasco sauce, optional
salt and pepper

Makes 200 ml/1 scant cup

Whisk all the ingredients together and season to taste.
    Serve this dressing with a grilled/broiled chicken salad made with butter lettuce.

green goddess

Invented in the 1920s and named after the famous movie of the time *The Green Goddess*, this mayonnaise-based dressing is, as the name suggests, tinted green by the inclusion of fresh herbs. It was an adaptation of the French 'sauce vert' and is commonly served with crab-based salads. You can use any combination of fresh herbs you like.

2 tablespoons chopped mixed fresh
   herbs, such as parsley, tarragon and chives
1 white anchovy fillet in oil, drained and chopped
1 spring onion/scallion, trimmed and chopped
1 small garlic clove, crushed
150 ml/²/₃ cup mayonnaise (see page 23)
2 tablespoons milk
1 tablespoon white wine vinegar
salt and pepper

Makes 250 ml/1 cup plus 1 tablespoon

Place all the ingredients in a blender and blend until smooth. Adjust seasoning to taste and serve with a shellfish and lettuce salad.

caesar

There are endless recipes for both Caesar salad and its dressing and almost every restaurant serves its own version. To my mind, the best dressing always includes egg, garlic, anchovies and grated Parmesan. I like it with a good tang of anchovy, but you should use as little or as much as you like.

1 egg
1 tablespoon white wine vinegar
2–4 anchovy fillets in oil, drained and chopped
1 garlic clove, crushed
1 teaspoon Worcestershire sauce
125 ml/¹/₂ cup extra virgin olive oil
3 tablespoons freshly grated Parmesan
salt and pepper

Makes 175 ml/³/4 cup

Boil the egg for 3 minutes, then immediately plunge into cold water. Shell the egg and place in a blender. Add the vinegar, anchovies, garlic, Worcestershire sauce and a little salt and pepper and blend until frothy. Gradually whisk in the oil in a steady stream until the sauce is thickened. Stir in the Parmesan cheese and adjust seasoning to taste.

Serve drizzled over a cos lettuce, crouton, anchovy and Parmesan salad – if you like, you can add crispy fried bacon as well.

wedges of cos or lettuce with
blue cheese dressing

blue cheese

A classic dressing for wedges of chilled cos
or iceberg lettuce – you can experiment with
different types of blue cheese to give you the
flavour that works best for you. Here I have
used a creamy St Agur, which has a milder
taste than gorgonzola or Roquefort, but really
it's up to you.

75 ml/¹/₃ cup sour cream
50 g/¹/₄ cup creamy blue cheese
1 tablespoon white wine vinegar
2 teaspoons just-boiled water
2 tablespoons extra virgin olive oil
1 tablespoon chopped fresh chives
salt and pepper

Makes approximately 200 ml/1 scant cup

Place the sour cream, cheese, vinegar, water and
a little salt and pepper in a blender and blend until
fairly smooth. Add the oil and blend again. Stir in
the chives, adjust seasoning to taste and serve.

This creamy dressing, with its lovely tang of
acidity from the blue cheese, is wonderful with cos or
iceberg lettuce. It also works well with all green leaf
salads, celery, apple, pear and mixed nuts.

goat's cheese and basil

A creamy dressing with a tang of goat's cheese
makes a delicious foil for a salad of mixed
tomatoes. It could also be used as an alternative
to a Caesar dressing on a salad of crisp cos
lettuce, croutons and fried bacon bits.

100 g/scant ¹/₂ cup soft goat's cheese
4 tablespoons runny yogurt
2 tablespoons warm water
2 teaspoons white wine vinegar
1 tablespoon finely chopped basil
salt and pepper

Makes 200 ml/1 scant cup

Place the cheese, yogurt, water and vinegar in a
blender and blend until smooth. Add the basil and
blend again until the sauce is speckled and a pale
green colour. Season to taste and serve.

This dressing is perfect over a medley of different
varieties of tomatoes, pitted black olives and thinly
sliced red onion.

herbed labne

Labne (labneh or labni) is a thickened yogurt made by straining off the whey and is popular throughout the eastern Mediterranean and Middle East, where it is often served as part of a mezze. The straining process increases the fat content, giving labne a more creamy texture. It is often formed into small balls and stored in oil. It is available to buy from larger supermarkets and specialist food stores (you could use thick Greek yogurt in this recipe instead).

125 g/1/2 cup labne or thick Greek yogurt
2 tablespoons extra virgin olive oil
1 tablespoon chopped fresh herbs, such as
  coriander/cilantro, mint and parsley
2 teaspoons lemon juice
1/2 teaspoon clear honey
1/4 teaspoon smoked paprika
salt and pepper

Makes 200 ml/1 scant cup

Place all the ingredients in a blender and blend until smooth. Adjust seasoning to taste and serve.

Serve the dressing with a new potato, chicory, smoked salmon and beetroot/beet salad.

creamy russian

Despite its name, this dressing was invented in the US in the late 19th century and was thought to have originally included caviar, hence the name. Traditionally it was used in a Reuben sandwich, a hot corned beef and sauerkraut sandwich on rye bread. This version is made with sour cream instead of mayonnaise, but you could substitute mayo if you prefer.

150 ml/2/3 cup sour cream
1 tablespoon lemon juice
1 tablespoon hot chilli//chili sauce
1 tablespoon chopped white onion
2 teaspoons horseradish sauce
salt and pepper

Makes 250 ml/1 cup plus 1 tablespoon

Place all the ingredients in a bowl and stir well until evenly combined. Adjust seasoning to taste and serve.

This dressing is perfect served with rare sliced beef, thinly sliced onion and crisp salad leaves.

new potato, chicory, smoked salmon and beetroot/
beet salad with *herbed labne dressing*

avocado and tarragon

With its naturally smooth, velvety flesh, avocado is a superb addition to a creamy salad dressing.
It works well with lots of herbs but I particularly like pairing it with tarragon and this makes it the
perfect dressing for fish- or chicken-based salads – try it as an alterative dressing to a Caesar.

1 small avocado
125 ml/½ cup buttermilk
1 spring onion/scallion, finely
chopped
2 tablespoons chopped fresh
tarragon
2 tablespoons avocado oil
1½ tablespoons lemon juice
salt and pepper

Makes 300 ml/1¼ cups

Cut the avocado in half and remove the stone. Scoop the flesh into a blender
and add the buttermilk, spring onion/scallion, tarragon, oil, lemon juice and
a little salt and pepper and blend until smooth.

Thin with milk or water if necessary, adjust seasoning to taste and serve.

coconut and chilli

Coconut cream adds a light creaminess to this Asian-inspired dressing and is based on a salad dressing I had in Longrain in Sydney, one of the best and most renowned Thai restaurants in Australia.

1 tablespoon peanut oil
125 ml/½ cup coconut cream
1 tablespoon Thai fish sauce
grated zest and juice ½ lime
1 teaspoon grated root ginger
2 teaspoons clear honey
1 large red chilli/chile, seeded
and chopped
a little pepper

Makes 150 ml/⅔ cup

Whisk all the ingredients together except the chilli/chile, transfer to a bottle and add the chilli/chile. Adjust seasoning to taste and serve.

This is delicious served with char-grilled scallops or on a chicken and shredded vegetable salad.

louis

Traditionally served with crab, this creamy, tangy mayonnaise-based dressing was invented in San Francisco in the early 1900s, with two hotels laying claim to the recipe.

150 ml/²/₃ cup mayonnaise (see page 23)
2 teaspoons mild chilli/chile sauce
1 spring onion/scallion, finely chopped
1 tablespoon pitted green olives, finely chopped
grated zest and juice ¹/₂ lemon
1 teaspoon Worcestershire sauce
1 teaspoon horseradish sauce
salt and pepper

Makes 300 ml/1¹/₄ cups

Place all the ingredients in a bowl and whisk together until combined, adjust seasoning to taste and serve.

Serve with a salad of lettuce, tomatoes, celery, hard-boiled eggs and top with fresh crabmeat.

marie rose

Marie rose, that archetypal 70s prawn/shrimp cocktail dressing, in fact originates from the 60s and was (most likely) adapted from a far older recipe, thousand island dressing, which was first introduced in America in the 1900s by none other than renowned British cook, Fanny Craddock. Its ingredients centre around mayonnaise flavoured with tomato ketchup, Worcestershire sauce, lemon juice and pepper, but it can include Tabasco and orange juice amongst others. It should be drizzled over prawns/shrimp.

100 ml/¹/₃ cup plus 1 tablespoon mayonnaise (see page 23)
2 tablespoons tomato ketchup
1 teaspoon Worcestershire sauce
a squeeze of fresh lemon juice
ground white pepper

Makes 150 ml/²/₃ cup

Simply blend all ingredients together, serve immediately or store.

lettuce, tomatoes, celery and hard-
boiled eggs topped with fresh crabmeat
with *louis dressing*

*herbed
dressings*

coriander and toasted sesame

The toasted sesame seeds add a wonderfully nutty, smoky flavour to this Japanese-style dressing. It is delicious tossed through a mixed noodle and vegetable salad with avocado and tomatoes. If making ahead, make sure to give it a really good shake before using. This dressing is similar to the traditional Japanese dressing served over wilted spinach.

2 tablespoons sesame seeds
2 large spring onions/scallions, trimmed and chopped
I tablespoon chopped coriander/cilantro leaves
I teaspoon caster/superfine sugar
I tablespoon rice wine vinegar
I tablespoon light soy sauce
3 tablespoons sunflower oil
2 teaspoons sesame oil
salt and pepper

Makes 150 ml/⅔ cup

Dry fry the sesame seeds in a small fry pan over a medium heat until toasted and starting to release their aroma. Cool and transfer to a blender. Blend to a paste with the spring onions/scallions, coriander/cilantro, sugar, vinegar, soy sauce and a pinch of salt.

Add the oils and blend again until amalgamated. Adjust seasoning to taste and serve.

dill and orange with walnut oil

The combination of orange, dill and walnut oil is lovely and makes a wonderful dressing for smoked fish salads. You can vary the oil and use hazelnut or extra virgin olive oil, if preferred.

grated zest and juice I orange
I small shallot, finely chopped
I small garlic clove, crushed
I tablespoon red wine vinegar
4 tablespoons walnut oil
I tablespoon chopped fresh dill
salt and pepper

Makes 150 ml/⅔ cup

Place the orange zest and juice, shallot, garlic, vinegar and salt and pepper in a bowl and whisk together. Gradually whisk in the oil until the dressing is amalgamated. Stir in the dill and serve.

Serve over frisée lettuce leaves with flaked smoked trout, blanched fine green beans and lightly toasted chopped walnuts.

greek oregano

The beauty of travelling for me is to discover the tastes and flavours of other countries' cuisines and Greece will forever be about simple everyday ingredients transformed by the sun – big juicy tomatoes and sweet sliced onions topped with brilliant white feta and a scattering of dried rigani, or Greek oregano. In full bloom, it reaches almost half a metre (2 feet) in height and has small white flowers. It is cut and dried in long stalks, with the flowers often still attached, and it is universally considered the king of oregano. You can buy packets of rigani in specialist food stores.

6 tablespoons Kalamata olive oil
1 tablespoon red wine vinegar
2 teaspoons rigani or dried oregano
salt and pepper

Makes 75 ml/⅓ cup

Place all the ingredients in a screw top jar and shake well until amalgamated. Allow to rest for 30 minutes for the oregano to soften. Shake again and serve.

Serve with a classic Greek salad of tomatoes, onion, green or black olives and feta.

parsley and green olive

This dressing is similar to a salsa verde, or 'green sauce'. It is a vibrant green colour and is great stirred through a pasta and tomato salad.

3 tablespoons chopped parsley
10 pitted green olives, roughly chopped
½ shallot, chopped
1 small garlic clove, crushed
1 tablespoon white wine vinegar
125 ml/½ cup extra virgin olive oil
1 tablespoon hot water
salt and pepper

Makes 125 ml/½ cup

Place the parsley, olives, shallot, garlic, vinegar and a little salt and pepper in a blender and blend until fairly well chopped. Add the oil and water and blend again until you have a vibrant green sauce. Adjust seasoning to taste and serve.

I also like to serve this dressing with shredded cooked chicken, finely chopped spring onions/scallions, diced tomato and cooked bulgur wheat for a delicious and wholesome lunch.

greek salad with
greek oregano dressing

chive and shallot

Avocado oil has the most gorgeous deep green luminosity to it, making this a really striking-looking dressing. The flavour of avocado oil is milder than extra virgin olive oil and works really well with the shallot and chives in this dressing.

1 shallot, very finely chopped
1 tablespoon chopped fresh
  chives
1 small garlic clove, crushed
6 tablespoons avocado oil
1 tablespoon lemon juice
a good pinch of caster/
  superfine sugar
salt and pepper

Makes 125 ml/½ cup

Place all the ingredients in a jar, seal the lid and shake well until the dressing is amalgamated. Adjust seasoning to taste and serve.

Serve with a crisp bacon and cos lettuce salad with garlic croutons.

dill and horseradish

Use fresh horseradish if you can, as the flavour and texture of the root is superior to that found pre-grated in jars. Until grated the root itself has little aroma but, as soon as the flesh is damaged, the enzymes break down to produce a mustard oil. The grated flesh must be used immediately.

2–3 cm/1-inch piece of horseradish root, peeled (or 2 teaspoons grated horseradish)

1 tablespoon sour cream

1 tablespoon lemon juice

1 tablespoon chopped fresh dill

5 tablespoons extra virgin olive oil

salt and pepper

Makes 200 ml/ 1 scant cup

If using horseradish root, finely grate the flesh into a bowl (or simply spoon in 2 teaspoons of the grated horseradish) and stir in the sour cream, lemon juice, dill and a little salt and pepper. Then whisk in the oil until the dressing is thickened and smooth. Adjust seasoning to taste and serve.

This dressing is delicious with a smoked fish and beetroot/beet salad.

mexican lime, coriander and chipotle chilli

Chipotle chillies/chiles have a wonderfully smoky flavour and aroma, giving this dressing a wonderful rich quality. You can buy dried chipotle chillies/chiles if you prefer but the paste, available from specialist food stores, is perfect for dressings. Both agave syrup and pumpkin seed oil will be available in health food stores.

1–2 teaspoon dried chipotle chilli/chile paste
grated zest and juice 1 lime
1 teaspoon agave syrup
3 tablespoons pumpkin seed oil or avocado oil
1 tablespoon chopped fresh coriander/cilantro
salt and pepper

Makes 75 ml/⅓ cup

Combine the chilli/chile paste, lime zest and juice, agave syrup and a little salt and pepper in a bowl and whisk until smooth. Gradually whisk in the oil until smooth, stir in the coriander/cilantro and serve.

Try drizzling this dressing over a shredded chicken, corn and avocado salad on a warm tortilla.

mint salsa verde

Based on the classic Italian sauce, this dressing is thinned a little with boiling water to give a pouring consistency suitable to dress salads. It is best used straightaway while the mint remains a bright green colour, but if you want to make it ahead of time, omit the lemon juice until just before serving.

½ bunch fresh mint leaves, roughly chopped
1 garlic clove, crushed
1 tablespoon drained capers
2 pitted green olives, chopped
2 teaspoons lemon juice
½ teaspoon caster/superfine sugar
5 tablespoons extra virgin olive oil
1 tablespoon boiling water
salt and pepper

Makes 125 ml/½ cup

Place the mint leaves, garlic, capers, olives, lemon juice, sugar, salt and pepper in a blender and blend until as finely chopped as possible.

Add the oil and water and blend again until you have an evenly blended, vibrant green dressing. Adjust seasoning to taste.

This is fabulous poured over a char-grilled lamb salad with haricot beans, steamed potatoes and rocket/arugula leaves.

shredded chicken, corn and avocado
salad with tortilla and
*mexican lime, coriander
and chipotle chilli dressing*

fruity
dressings

pink grapefruit and peppercorn

This dressing is a pretty pale pink colour, speckled with the deeper pink of the crushed pink peppercorns. It has a sweet yet slightly bitter note from the grapefruit juice. Pink peppercorns are not actually the same as black pepper but were named so because of their strong resemblance to black peppercorns and their peppery flavour.

juice ¹/₂ ruby grapefruit, about 3 tablespoons
¹/₂ teaspoon pink peppercorns, freshly crushed
1 teaspoon caster/superfine sugar
¹/₂ teaspoon Dijon mustard
4 tablespoons extra virgin olive oil
1 tablespoon chopped fresh chervil (optional)
salt

Makes 125–150 ml/¹/₂–²/₃ cup

Place the grapefruit juice, peppercorns, sugar, mustard and a little salt (if using) in a bowl and whisk well, then gradually whisk in the oil until amalgamated. Add the chervil, if using. Adjust seasoning and serve.

Grapefruit works really well with strong-flavoured fish, such as mackerel, and would make the perfect dressing for a smoked mackerel, chicory/endive and grapefruit salad.

3 citrus

Combining three different citrus fruits in the one dressing is lovely and the addition of the grated zest deepens the intensity of the citrus flavour. You can either make your own lemon-flavoured oil (see page 51) or buy one from a specialist food store. Alternatively, this dressing is also good with a plain extra virgin olive oil.

grated zest and juice ¹/₂ lemon
grated zest and juice ¹/₂ lime
grated zest and juice ¹/₂ orange
1 teaspoon whole grain mustard
1–2 teaspoons soft brown sugar
5 tablespoons lemon-infused oil
salt and pepper

Makes 150 ml/²/₃ cup

Scrub the fruit well before grating the zest into a bowl. Add the juice of all three fruits and stir in the mustard, sugar and salt and pepper until the sugar is dissolved. Whisk in the oil until combined, adjust seasoning to taste and serve.

This dressing is fabulous drizzled over a shaved fennel, lobster or prawn/shrimp and chervil salad with a few segments of orange.

key west mango and lime

Mango flesh provides a great base for this pretty dressing, but you will need to buy a ripe mango. The dressing is perfect for serving with cooked prawns/shrimp and would make a great alternative sauce for a prawn/shrimp cocktail with avocado and lettuce.

1 small ripe mango, peeled, stoned and diced
grated zest and juice 2 small limes
2 teaspoons clear honey
3 tablespoons avocado oil
1 red chilli/chile, seeded and finely chopped
salt and pepper

Makes 150 ml/⅔ cup

Place the mango in a blender with the lime zest, juice, honey and a little salt and pepper and blend until smooth, add the oil and blend again. Transfer to a bowl and stir in the chilli/chile. Adjust seasoning to taste and serve.

maple syrup, apple and walnut

This fruity, nutty dressing with a caramel flavour imparted from the maple syrup is really versatile. Walnut vinegar is a relatively recent addition to the wide variety of commercial vinegars. If unavailable, cider vinegar makes a good alternative.

2 tablespoons clear apple juice
1 tablespoon walnut vinegar or cider vinegar
2 teaspoons maple syrup
1 teaspoon whole grain mustard
3 tablespoons walnut oil
1 tablespoon extra virgin olive oil
salt and pepper

Makes 100 ml/⅓ cup plus 1 tablespoon

Place the apple juice, vinegar, maple syrup and mustard in a bowl with a little salt and pepper and whisk together until smooth. Then gradually whisk in the two oils until emulsified. Adjust seasoning to taste and serve.

Crumble some goat's cheese over rocket/arugula leaves and top with thinly sliced apple, toasted walnuts, shaved Parmesan and a good drizzle of dressing.

prawn/shrimp cocktail with
key west mango and lime

preserved lemon

This salty-sour dressing with a hint of sweetness is a real winner and is fantastic served with a crisp green leaf salad or stirred through a chicken couscous salad. Preserved lemons are now readily available and should be found in larger supermarkets; alternatively try Middle Eastern food stores and delis.

4 tablespoons extra virgin olive oil
I tablespoon preserved lemon, diced
I garlic clove, crushed
I tablespoon lemon juice
2 teaspoons clear honey
I tablespoon chopped fresh coriander/cilantro
salt and pepper

Makes 150 ml/⅔ cup

Combine all the ingredients in a blender and blend until smooth and vibrant green.

Drizzle over a salad of couscous, shredded grilled/broiled chicken, tomatoes and fresh spring onions/scallions.

homemade pomegranate syrup

This syrup is the most stunning deep pink colour and has a wonderfully fruity flavour. It is a great addition to a salad dressing and can be stored for up to 1 week in the fridge and used to drizzle on ice cream or yogurt, too.

175 ml/³/₄ cup fresh pomegranate juice (2 large pomegranates)

125 g/4¹/₂ oz. caster/superfine sugar

1 tablespoon lemon juice

1 teaspoon Dijon mustard

5 tablespoons extra virgin olive oil

salt and pepper

Makes 125 ml/ ¹/₂ cup

To make the juice, lightly bash the pomegranates on a board then cut in half, holding them over a bowl to catch the juices. Scoop out all the seeds and flesh into the bowl and pass through a sieve/strainer. You should have about 175 ml /³/₄ cup of juice.

Place the pomegranate juice and sugar in a small saucepan and heat gently, stirring until the sugar is dissolved. Increase the heat and simmer for 15 minutes until the juice is syrup-like and reduced to about 125 ml/¹/₂ cup. Set aside to cool completely.

Combine 2 tablespoons of the cooled syrup with the lemon juice, mustard and a little salt and pepper and gradually whisk in the oil until emulsified. Adjust seasoning to taste.

This dressing is great served with a Parma ham and melon salad or any combination of cured meat and fruit.

peach salsa

This dish was inspired by a delicious salsa served to me by friends. I absolutely loved the combination of fruit and vanilla with a savoury dish. You can use whatever fruit is available really. Here I have used white flesh peaches as they were at their best as I was testing the recipe, but you could use pitted cherries, raspberries or strawberries with great effect.

1 small shallot, finely chopped
seeds from 1/2 vanilla bean
juice 1/2 orange
2 teaspoons sherry vinegar
5 tablespoons extra virgin olive oil
1 ripe white flesh peach, seeded and diced
1 tablespoon chopped fresh mint
salt and pepper
Makes 275 ml/1 cup plus 2 tablespoons

Whisk together the shallot, vanilla seeds, orange juice and vinegar and then gradually whisk in the oil until amalgamated. Stir in the peach and fresh mint and season to taste with salt and pepper.

Serve this dressing over a salad of duck breast, mixed leaves and fine green beans.

raspberry, mustard and honey

I love fruit-based dressings; I think it's because I like to combine sweet flavours with savoury ones. When fresh raspberries are out of season or unavailable you can easily use frozen raspberries, thawed.

100 g/3 1/2 oz. fresh raspberries
1 tablespoon red wine vinegar
1 tablespoon clear honey
2 teaspoons whole grain mustard
4 tablespoons extra virgin olive oil
salt and pepper
Makes 175 ml/3/4 cup

Place the raspberries, vinegar, honey, mustard and a little salt and pepper in a blender and blend until smooth. Transfer to a bowl and whisk in the oil until evenly blended. Adjust seasoning to taste.

Serve with a smoked duck or smoked chicken and leaf salad.

Variation: You can replace the raspberries with other soft fruit, such as strawberries or blueberries with equal success. Pair strawberries with hazelnut oil and blueberries with a tarragon vinegar.

duck breast, mixed leaves
and fine green beans with
peach salsa

*infused
dressings*

lemon, olive and pepper

The oil is infused with lemon zest and slices, crushed olives and peppercorns for a few days, allowing the flavours to permeate the oil. The oil is then strained ready for vinegar or lemon juice to be added.

1 lemon
8 large pitted green olives, sliced
1/2 teaspoon each black and pink peppercorns, bruised
150 ml/2/3 cup extra virgin olive oil
lemon juice, to taste
salt

Makes 150 ml/2/3 cup

Thinly pare the zest from the lemon and then, using a sharp knife, cut away the pith from the whole lemon. Cut the lemon into thin slices. Place the zest and slices in a jar with the olives and peppercorns (bashed slightly), pour over the oil and allow to infuse for 5 days.

Strain off and discard the flavourings and pour the oil into a bowl. Whisk in enough lemon juice for your taste and adjust seasoning to taste.

Drizzle over tomatoes or a tuna and bean salad.

bay and thyme

Bay and thyme give the oil a delicious mellow flavour and, once strained, it is perfectly enhanced with a light vinegar, such as Chinese black vinegar or rice wine vinegar.

6 bay leaves
4 sprigs fresh thyme
salt and pepper
150 ml/2/3 cup extra virgin olive oil
1–2 tablespoons vinegar of your choice

Makes 200 ml/1 scant cup

Place the bay leaves, thyme, salt and pepper in a pestle and mortar and pound gently to bash up the herbs. Transfer to a jar, add the oil and marinate for 5 days.

Strain the oil into a jar, add vinegar, salt and pepper to taste and serve.

This dressing is great served over salad leaves or shaved courgettes/zucchini.

smoked garlic oil

Tea-smoking is a terrific way to flavour foods with a rich and intense smoke flavour. It is often used to smoke salmon or duck, but works well here with the garlic. You will need to double line the wok with foil and it's a good idea to open a window when you are smoking foods as the aroma is quite pungent.

**8 tablespoons soft brown
    sugar**

8 tablespoons long grain rice

8 tablespoons tea leaves

I head garlic

**250 ml/I cup plus I tablespoon
    extra virgin olive**

**vinegar or lemon juice, to
    taste**

salt and pepper

Makes 300 ml/1¼ cups

Line a wok with a double sheet of foil and combine the brown sugar, rice and tea leaves in the bottom. Place a small rack or griddle over the smoking mixture (making sure the two don't touch) and lay the garlic on the rack.

Place the wok over a high heat and, as soon as the mixture starts to smoke, top the wok with a tight-fitting lid. Lower the heat and cook gently for 15 minutes until the garlic turns a deep brown. Allow to cool.

Place the unpeeled garlic in a bottle or jar, add the oil and allow to infuse for 1 week. Drain and use the oil to make a dressing, adding vinegar or lemon juice to taste. Great with a beef carpaccio or a charred lamb salad.

saffron oil

The saffron adds both a pretty colour and a delightfully delicate flavour to the dressing, which is delicious when drizzled over a mixed leaf and tomato salad.

a large pinch of saffron strands
1 tablespoon white wine vinegar
1 teaspoon caster/superfine sugar
4 tablespoons extra virgin olive oil
salt and pepper

Makes 100 ml/⅓ cup plus 1 tablespoon

Place the saffron, 1 tablespoon water, vinegar and sugar in a small saucepan and heat gently, stirring until the sugar is dissolved. Bring to the boil and remove from the heat. Set aside to cool completely. Add the oil, season to taste and serve.

piri-piri

This is a classic Portuguese dressing traditionally drizzled over char-grilled chicken. The dressing packs a powerful punch, despite the fact that it uses only 8 small dried red chillies/chiles (traditionally African bird's eye chillies/chiles are used in Portugal). Look out for the Italian dried pepperoncino chillies/chiles.

8 small dried red chillies/chiles
250 ml/1 cup plus 1 tablespoon extra virgin olive oil
2 garlic cloves, crushed
grated zest 1 lemon
2 tablespoons white wine vinegar
salt and pepper

Makes 300 ml/1¼ cups

Finely chop the chillies/chiles and place in a small bottle, top up with the oil and leave to infuse for 1–2 weeks. Add the garlic, lemon zest, vinegar and a little salt and pepper, shake well and serve.

As well as over grilled chicken this dressing is also fabulous over char-grilled calamari/squid, prawns/shrimp and sardines.

basil oil

This dressing is not only a beautiful colour, but is also really fragrant with pungent fresh basil leaves. It is best made in the summer months when basil is at its prime and, of course, most inexpensive.

25 g/¾ oz. fresh basil leaves
300 ml/1¼ cup extra virgin olive oil
a little lemon juice
a pinch of salt

Makes 100 ml/⅓ cup plus 1 tablespoon

Blend the basil leaves, oil and a little salt in a blender to make a vivid green paste. Allow to infuse overnight and the next day strain the oil through a layer of muslin/cheesecloth. Store the oil in the fridge, returning to room temperature before use.

This dressing is best served with lemon juice but, rather than mixing the juice into the oil, add it directly to the salad.

Arrange a plate of heirloom tomatoes and drizzle over some basil oil, squeeze with a little lemon juice and serve.

char-grilled chicken
with *piri piri*

warm dressings

greek island

With flavours reminiscent of holidays spent on the Greek islands, this dressing is delicious drizzled over a grilled/broiled lamb salad with white beans, char-grilled courgettes/zucchini and black olives.

6 tablespoons extra virgin olive oil
1/2 red onion, finely chopped
1 garlic clove, crushed
grated zest and juice 1/2 lemon
a pinch of dried chilli/red pepper flakes
2 teaspoons chopped fresh rosemary
1 teaspoon chopped fresh thyme
1 small tomato, peeled, seeded and diced
salt and pepper

Makes 150 ml/2/3 cup

Heat 2 tablespoons of the oil and gently fry the onion, garlic, lemon zest, chilli/red pepper flakes and herbs with a little salt and pepper for 5 minutes until softened.

Stir in the lemon juice and whisk in the remaining oil. Remove the pan from the heat, stir in the tomato and adjust seasoning to taste. Serve immediately.

onion and moroccan spice

This is a super dressing for a chickpea salad with shredded chicken, raisins, tomatoes, toasted almonds and chopped fresh herbs. The syrup is the one from page 47 (or, if you like a more tart flavour, you could use pomegranate molasses with 1/2 teaspoon clear honey).

5 tablespoons argan or olive oil
1/2 small onion, thinly sliced
1 garlic clove, crushed
1 teaspoon Moroccan spice mix
2 teaspoons pomegranate syrup (see page 47)
1 tablespoon finely sliced preserved lemon
1 tablespoon red wine vinegar
salt and pepper

Makes 150 ml/2/3 cup

Heat 2 tablespoons of the oil in a small frying pan/skillet and gently fry the onion, garlic, spice mix and a little salt and pepper over a low heat for 5 minutes. Stir in the pomegranate syrup and warm through.

Remove the pan from the heat and whisk in the remaining oil. Stir in the preserved lemon and adjust seasoning to taste. Serve immediately.

black bean and ginger

This pungent dressing really packs a punch with its salty beans, ginger and chilli/chile. Salted black beans are available either vacuum packed or in cans from Asian food stores.

2 tablespoons salted black beans
3 tablespoons sunflower oil
I large red chilli/chile, seeded and chopped
I garlic clove, thinly sliced
I teaspoon grated root ginger
I tablespoon black vinegar or rice wine vinegar
3 tablespoons Chinese rice wine
2 teaspoons light soy sauce
I teaspoon clear honey

Makes 200 ml/1 scant cup

Soak the salted beans in cold water for 30 minutes, drain well and pat dry.

Heat the oil in a small frying pan/skillet and gently fry the chilli/chile, garlic and ginger over a low heat for 3–4 minutes until softened. Add the black beans, vinegar, rice wine, soy sauce and honey and warm through.

Serve warm drizzled over a charred pork, noodle and sugar snap pea salad.

mirin

This is a mildly flavoured Japanese-style dressing with a little sweetness from the mirin, balanced beautifully with the rice wine vinegar. It is lovely served warm poured over oysters on the half shell or over grilled scallops.

50 ml/3 ¹/₂ tablespoons mirin
I spring onion/scallion, trimmed and thinly sliced
I garlic clove, sliced
2 tablespoons rice wine vinegar
I tablespoon dark soy sauce
2 tablespoons peanut or sunflower oil
I tablespoon chopped fresh coriander/cilantro

Makes 150 ml/²/₃ cup

Place the mirin, half the spring onion/scallion, the garlic, vinegar and soy sauce in a small saucepan. Bring to the boil and simmer gently for 2 minutes. Strain the liquid through a sieve/strainer and set aside to cool to slightly.

Whisk in the oil, stir in the chopped coriander/cilantro and remaining spring onion/scallion and serve immediately.

charred pork, noodle and sugar snap peas
with *black bean and ginger*

sherry, orange and raisin

Pedro Ximenez is an intensely sweet dessert sherry made from grapes grown throughout Spain. In South America it is known as Pedro Gimenez. If unavailable, you could use Marsala or an alcohol-free alternative, such as raisin juice.

2 tablespoons extra virgin olive oil

30 g/1 oz. blanched whole hazelnuts

30 g/1 oz. raisins

3 tablespoons Pedro Ximenez, sweet sherry or raisin juice

2 tablespoons sherry vinegar

grated zest and juice 1 orange, about 3¹/₂ tablespoons

4 tablespoons hazelnut oil

salt and pepper

Makes 200 ml/1 scant cup

Heat the olive oil in a frying pan/skillet and gently fry the hazelnuts for 1–2 minute until golden, add the raisins and fry for a further 1 minute until soft.

Add the sherry and sherry vinegar to the pan and bubble for 30 seconds. Whisk in the orange zest and juice and warm through, then remove from the heat and transfer to a bowl.

Gradually whisk in the hazelnut oil, season to taste and serve warm with a salad of duck, chicory/endive and orange segments.

lemon, honey and shallot

The zing of lemon balanced with sweet honey combines to make a delicious dressing. Warm dressings are ideally suited to serving with cooked meat and fish-based salads and this one is especially good drizzled over char-grilled chicken and a mixed green salad.

6 tablespoons extra virgin olive oil

grated zest and juice 1 large lemon

1 garlic clove, crushed

1 small shallot, finely diced

1 large red chilli/chile, seeded and finely chopped

1 teaspoon cumin seeds, crushed

2 teaspoons clear honey

salt and pepper

Makes 250 ml/1 cup plus 1 tablespoon

Heat half the oil in a frying pan/skillet and gently fry the lemon zest, garlic, shallot, chilli/chile, cumin seeds and a little salt and pepper over a very low heat for 2–3 minutes until soft but not golden.

Add the lemon juice and honey and stir well. Remove the pan from the heat and pour into a bowl. Whisk in the remaining oil, season to taste and serve warm over your chosen salad.

caramelized garlic

The garlic is braised in olive oil until softened, resulting in a sweet garlic paste. This is then blended with the remaining ingredients, making a lovely creamy dressing. It needs to be used immediately as if it sits it will separate.

1 head garlic
125 ml/½ cup extra virgin olive oil
2 tablespoons white wine vinegar
salt and pepper

Makes 200 ml/1 scant cup

Peel the garlic cloves and place them in a small saucepan and cover with the oil. Heat gently and cook over a low heat for 20 minutes until the garlic is really softened.

Strain the oil into a jug/pitcher and transfer the garlic to a blender, add the vinegar, salt and pepper and blend until smooth. Gradually whisk in the oil until the dressing is emulsified.

This can be used as an alternative to a Caesar dressing, drizzled over mixed leaves, croutons and crispy fried bacon.

smoked chilli

Ancho chilli/chile is the name given to a poblano chilli/chile when it's dried and means 'wide' in Spanish, as it becomes flat and wide as it dries. It has a mellow, sweet aroma, giving this dressing a distinctive flavour and deep red colour.

1 dried ancho chilli/chile
300 ml/1¼ cups boiling water
2 tablespoons sunflower oil
1 spring onion/scallion, finely sliced
1 garlic clove, crushed
grated zest and juice 1 lime
2 teaspoons agave syrup
2 tablespoons pumpkin seed oil
salt and pepper

Makes 150 ml/⅔ cup

Place the chilli/chile in a bowl, cover with the boiling water and allow to soak for 15 minutes until softened. Cut in half and discard seeds and stalk. Finely chop the flesh and set aside.

Heat the sunflower oil in a small saucepan and gently fry the spring onion/scallion and garlic for 3 minutes until softened. Add the chilli/chile, lime zest and juice and agave syrup and warm through. Remove the pan from the heat, stir in the pumpkin oil until evenly blended and season to taste.

Serve drizzled over a grilled sweetcorn salad.

mixed leaves, croutons and
crispy fried bacon with
caramelized garlic

index